Survival
Italian

Buon Giorno,

We are pleased that you want to start learning Italian and intend to travel to Italy. Many tourists visit Italy every year because they love **il vino, il sole, l'arte** and much more.

Knowing a little Italian will help you understand and be understood in typical situations - and your attempts to speak Italian will be appreciated by everyone you encounter.

This entertaining and informative approach to the language does not require you to "cram" vocabulary and "slave over" grammar, as in school. It does not prepare you for a test, but rather is simply meant to afford you greater pleasure on your vacation, without requiring much effort. Make yourself comfortable, pick up a pencil. You will see that learning Italian can be very enjoyable.

So you can get right into the swing of things, we have prepared cartoon balloons for you to fill in. Each blank stands for one letter.

And now we will introduce a few important words. The pronunciation is in square brackets:

Buon giorno	[boo•ōn jō′rnō]	*Hello*
Per favore	[per fävō′re]	*Please*
Grazie	[grä′tsye]	*Thank you*
Si	[sē]	*Yes*
No	[nō]	*No*

Buon giorno literally means good day. Italians use it both in greeting and parting. It can therefore mean hello and goodbye, much as the less formal, Ciao, used among friends.

vō'lō	il volo	*flight*
pär'te	parte	*it leaves*
bēlye'tō	il biglietto	*ticket*
skōntre'nō	lo scontrino	*baggage receipt*
bägä'lyō	il bagaglio	*suitcase*
kōo•än'te bägä'lyē ä	quanti bagagli ha?	*How many bags do you have?*
päsäpōr'tō	il passaporto	*passport*
ä ke ōrä	a che ora?	*At what time?*
dä kōoä'le pōr'tä	de quale porta?	*From which gate?*
dälä pōr'tä nōo'merō dōo'e	dalla porta numero due	*from gate number 2*
me fä'tshä ved'ere	mi faccia vedere	*may I see*
sōo•ō	suo	*your*
sōo•ō päsäpōr'tō	il suo passaporto	*your passport*
e'kō	ecco	*here is*
ō dōoe	ho due	*I have two*
nōo'merō se'dētshē	numero sedici	*number sixteen*
per	per	*for*
bōo•ōn jō'rnō	buon giorno	*good day*
per fävō're	per favore	*please*
grä'tsye	grazie	*thank you*

Gender of Nouns

The Italian noun is either masculine of feminine. The definite article corresponding to "the" is **il** or **lo** (m.) or **la** or **l'** (f.). For a more detailed description of the articles, see page 35.

Nouns ending in		Example
o	masculine	abit**o** (suit)
a	feminine	post**a** (mail, post office)
e	masculine	calor**e** (heat)
	or feminine	chiav**e** (key)

Plural of Nouns

Nouns ending in **-o**, **-e** end in **-i** in the plural, nouns ending in **-a** end in **-e** in the plural.

9

1 Airport

NOTE: Answers for the dialogues in each chapter can be found starting on page 76.

2 Car   Macchina

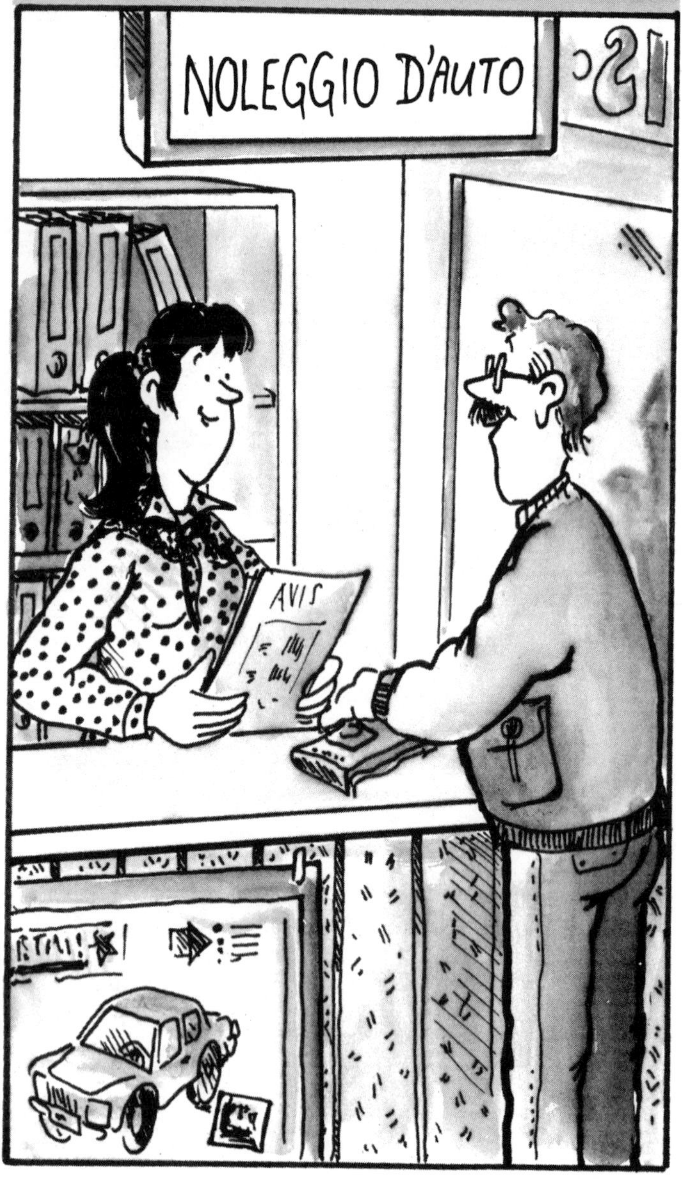

ōōna mä′kēnä	una macchina	car
ke tēpō dē	che tipo de	What type of
mä′kēnä	macchina?	car?
ōōna dē lōōsō	(una di) lusso	luxury
ōōna pōr′tä	una porta	door
ä kōō•ätrō pōr′te	a quattro porte	four-door
ä dōō′e pōr′te	a due porte	two-door
nōlejä′re	noleggiare	to rent
vōre′e	vorrei	I'd like
vōre′be	vorrebbe	you'd like
kōō•äntō kōstä	quanto costa?	How much does it cost?
lē′re	lire	lire
tshentōmē′lä	centomila	100,000
dōō•etshentōmē′lä	duecentomila	200,000
ōōn mēlyō′ne	un milione	1,000,000
lä pren′dō	la prendo	I'll take it
per kōō•än′tō	per quanto	For how
tem′pō	tempo?	long?
per ōōnä setēm′änä	per una settimana	for one week
kēlō′metre	chilometre	unlimited
ēlemēta′te	illimitati	mileage
be′ne	bene	fine, o.k.
sē	si	yes

Tolls

On highways, a toll (**pedaggio**) that can be quite expensive is collected.

2 Car

Organize a trip from *Milano* to *Roma*. You may wish to consult a road map or atlas.

——————, ——————, ——————, *Roma*,
——————, ——————, ——————, ——————.

I'll ask if we can get a room in this hotel.*

kä′merä	la camera	room
ä oo′nä kä′merä lē′berä	ha una camera libera?	Do you have a room available?
oo′nä do′pyä	una doppia	double room
tshen′tō mē′lä	centomila	one hundred thousand
jō′rnō per tshen′kooe jo′rne	il giorno per cinque giorni	day for five days
tem′pō	il tempo	time
boo•onä se′rä	buona sera	good evening
sēnyōr′, sēnyōr′e	signor, signore	sir, mister, Mr.
sēnyōr′ä	signora	madam, Mrs.

Signor(e)

Signore stands alone, **Signor,** in front of names. For example: **Signor** Ponti. The feminine, **Signora** does not change: **Signora** Ponti.

Hotel Listings

Hotels are divided into five categories. There is a hotel listing for many cities, regions and provinces (**elenco degli alberghi**).

Campgrounds

In Italy there are over 1,500 campgrounds. Camping on private property is allowed only with the owner's permission.

---

* The balloons at the beginning of each lesson are illustrations only and do not require you to translate them.

3 Hotel

5 Five
6 Room
7 Lira
8 Okay

1 Day
2 How much
3 Time
4 Evening

19

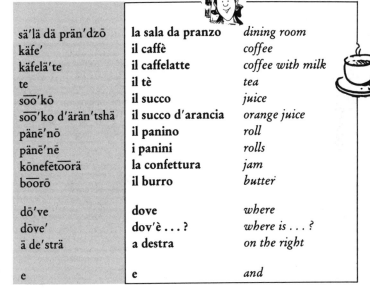

sä'lä dä prän'dzō	**la sala da pranzo**	*dining room*
käfe'	**il caffè**	*coffee*
käfelä'te	**il caffelatte**	*coffee with milk*
te	**il tè**	*tea*
sōō'kō	**il succo**	*juice*
sōō'ko d'ärän'tshä	**il succo d'arancia**	*orange juice*
pänē'nō	**il panino**	*roll*
pänē'nē	**i panini**	*rolls*
kōnefētōōrä	**la confettura**	*jam*
bōōrō	**il burro**	*butter*
dō've	**dove**	*where*
dōve'	**dov'è . . . ?**	*where is . . . ?*
ä de'strä	**a destra**	*on the right*
e	**e**	*and*

Breakfast (**la colazione**) in Italy usually consists of no more than coffee and a roll with jam and butter, or a danish.

4 Breakfast

Colazione 4

23

In the morning a visit
to the Uffizi.
In the afternoon . . .

pyän'tä	la pianta	*map*
ōōnä pyän'tä de'lä tshētä	una pianta della città	*a map of the city*
pyä'tsä	la piazza	*square*
pyä'tsä de'lä sēnyōrē'ä	Piazza della Signoria	*Signoria square*
ä'lä pyä'tsä de'lä sēnyōrē'ä	alla Piazza della Signoria	*to Signoria square*
ōōn au'tōbōōs	un autobus	*a bus*
pren'dere	prendere	*to take*
le'ē pōō•ō'	Lei può	*You can*
pren'dere	prendere	*take*
ōōn au'tōbōōs	un autobus	*a bus*
kōō•e'stō au'tōbōōs	questo autobus	*this bus*
kōō•e'stō au'tōbōōs vä	questo autobus va . . .	*this bus goes to . . .*
vōre'ē	vorrei	*I would like*
mē'le grätsye	mille grazie	*thank you very much*
dē nyen'te	di niente	*don't mention it*
skōō'zē	scusi	*excuse me*
nōn lō sō	non lo so	*I don't know*
gälerē'ä de'lyē ōōfētsē	la galleria degli Uffizi	*The Uffizi Gallery*
bēlye'tō	il biglietto	*ticket*

Galleria degli Uffizi

This is one of the world's greatest museums; with more than 4,000 paintings by Botticelli, Leonardo da Vinci, Raffaello, Michelangelo, Titian and others.

Many museums are only open until noon. Most of them are closed on Mondays.

25

5 Museum

5 Museum

ōon espre′sō	un expresso	*an espresso*
ōo′nä sēgäre′tä	una sigaretta	*a cigarette*
ō′jē	oggi	*today*
kăl′dō	caldo	*hot*
fä mōl′tō käl′dō	fa molto caldo	*it's very hot*
lētälyä′	l'Italia	*Italy*
lyē stä′tē ōōnē′tē	gli Stati Uniti	*the United States*
ämerēkä′nō,	americano,	*American*
ämerēkä′nä	americana	
sō′nō	sono	*I am, they are*
di nyōō yōrk	di New York	*from New York*
änke	anche	*also, so is, too*
mē pyätshe′	mi piace	*I like*
bello, bella	bello, bella	*handsome, beautiful*
vē′no	il vino	*wine*
sō′le	il sole	*sun*
lä′rte	l'arte	*art*

---

* "Venus of Urbino" is a famous painting by Titian (1477–1576).

31

6 A coffee

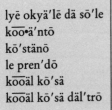

lyē okyä'lē dä sō'le	**gli occhiali da sole**	*sun glasses*
kōō•ä'ntō	**quanto**	*How much do*
kō'stänō	**costano . . . ?**	*(they) cost . . . ?*
le pren'dō	**li prendo**	*I'll take them*
kōōäl kō'sä	**qualcosa**	*something*
kōōäl kō'sä däl'trō	**qualcosa d'altro**	*something else*
mōne'tä	**la moneta**	*coin*
kämbyä're	**cambiare**	*to exchange*
kämbyä're sōl'dē	**cambiare soldi**	*to exchange money*
dōve' pōtre'ē	**dove potrei**	*Where can I*
kämbyä're	**cambiare?**	*exchange?*
dō'lärē	**dollari**	*dollars*
tretshentō-	**trecento-**	*three hundred*
nōväntämē'lä	**novantamila**	*ninety thousand*
lē're	**lire**	*lire*
tshēnkōō•än'tä- mē'lä	**cinquantamila**	*fifty thousand*
lä	**là**	*over there*
nō	**no**	*no*

Singular articles
Masculine: **il, l'** (before a vowel), **lo** (before s followed by a consonant or a word beginning with z).
Feminine: **la, l'** (before a vowel).

Plural articles
Masculine: **i, gli** (before a vowel, s + consonant and z).
Feminine: **le**.

Banks
Banks are open Monday to Friday from 8:30 A.M. to 12:30 P.M. and for one hour in the afternoon. You must have your passport with you in order to exchange money.

7 Exchange

36

7 Exchange

→
7 Passport

↓ 1 Thing
2 Italian currency
3 Bank
4 Exchange
5 Coin
6 I would like

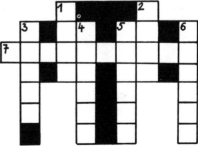

kärtōlē′nä	la cartolina	postcard
kōō•e′ste kärtōlē′ne	queste cartoline	these postcards
fränkōbō′lō	il francobollo	stamp
tshēn′kōō•e	cinque	five stamps
fränkōbō′lē	francobolli	
per lyē stätē ōōnēttē	per gli Stati Uniti	for the U.S.
pōs′tä	la posta	mail, post office
dōō•emē′lä	duemila	two thousand
tshēn′kōō•etshentō	cinquecento-	five hundred
tshēnkōō•än′tä	cinquanta	fifty

Mailboxes

When sending mail, note the indications **PER LA CITTA** (local) and **PER TUTTE LE ALTRE DESTINAZIONI** (out of town).

Stamps

You can buy stamps at the Post Office or tobacco store (**Tabacchi**). **Tabacchi** are easily identified by a large black letter "T" on a white background affixed to the storefront. Bus tickets may also be purchased here, by the unit or by groups of ten.

8 Postcards

Cartoline 8

→
4 Stamp

↓
1 Postcard
2 Also, too
3 Post Office

43

44

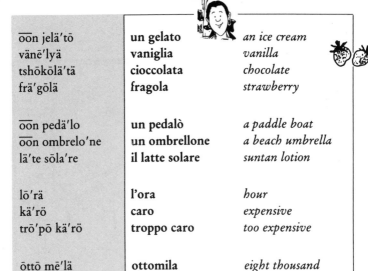

ōōn jelä′tō	un gelato	an ice cream
vänē′lyä	vaniglia	vanilla
tshōkōlä′tä	cioccolata	chocolate
frä′gōlä	fragola	strawberry
ōōn pedä′lo	un pedalò	a paddle boat
ōōn ombrelo′ne	un ombrellone	a beach umbrella
lä′te sōla′re	il latte solare	suntan lotion
lō′rä	l'ora	hour
kä′rō	caro	expensive
trō′pō kä′rō	troppo caro	too expensive
ōttō mē′lä	ottomila	eight thousand
tren′tä mē′lä	trentamila	thirty thousand

Beaches

Most Italian bathing beaches are divided into small lots which belong to private individuals. Tourists must pay admission and can use cabanas or showers.

Popular beaches are especially crowded during the two week period around August 15th (**il Ferragosto**).

45

9 At the Beach

9 At the Beach

1 Ice cream
2 Beach
3 Vanilla
6 Chocolate

4 Beach umbrella
5 Suntan lotion
6 Expensive

desē′derä	desidera?	*What would you like?*
ärän′tshä	l'arancia	*orange*
tshēn′koo•e arän′tshe	cinque arance	*five oranges*
pōmōdō′rō	il pomodoro	*tomato*
oon kēlō de pōmōdō′rē	un chilo di pomodori	*a kilo of tomatoes*
ensälä′ta de pōmōdō′rē	l'insalata di pomodori	*tomato salad*
bänänä	la banana	*banana*
bänänē sō′nō mōl′tō boo•ōne	le banane sono molto buone	*the bananas are very good*
ä′lyō	l'aglio	*garlic*
äbyä′mō delä′lyō	abbiamo dell'aglio	*we have some garlic*
lä′lyō e mōl′tō boo•ōnō	l'aglio è molto buono	*the garlic is very good*
koo•ē′	qui	*here*
per	per	*for*

Business Hours

Business hours are generally from 8:30 or 9:30 A.M. to 1:00 P.M. and from 4:30 P.M. to 7:30 or 8:00 P.M.

In Italy, the midday break may last up to 4 hours, so it is best to run errands around town in the morning or late afternoon.

Amounts

Remember that in Italy the metric system is used and one calculates only in grams (**il grammo**) and kilograms (**il chilogrammo**). For example, in a store one would buy **un etto** (100g) or **due etti** (200g), **mezzo chilo** (500g) or **un chilo** (1,000g).

10 Fruit

prōn'tō	**pronto**	*hello*
pärlō	**parlo**	*I am speaking*
kōn kē pärlō	**con chi parlo?**	*Who's speaking?*
nō'me	**il nome**	*name*
el mē•ō nō'me	**il mio nome**	*my name*
ēl soo'ō nō'me	**il suo nome**	*your name*
tä'vōlä	**la tavola**	*table*
oonä tä'vōlä per	**una tavola per**	*a table for*
doo'e persō'ne	**due persone**	*two*
rēservä're	**riservare**	*to reserve*
dōmä'nē	**domani**	*tomorrow*
per dōmä'nē sē'rä	**per domani sera**	*for tomorrow night*

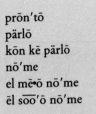

Telephone tokens

For many public phones you need Italian telephone tokens (**get-toni**). They can be purchased at the Post Office, from vending machines, at the **Tabacchi**, or in many bars where public phones can be found. During a call, when you hear a short signal you must press the button to drop another **gettone** in the telephone, or add more **gettoni** and press the button. Unused **gettoni** are returned at the end of the call.

Calling Home

The least expensive way to call home is to call from the SIP telephone offices in many cities or the Post Office. Here, you place your call at a counter and are directed to a booth (**cabina**) where you can speak to your party. Payment is made at the end of your call. You can also place a call through your hotel switchboard but hotels usually charge a fee for such a service.

11 Reservations

→
4 Evening
6 Table
7 Tomorrow
8 Name

↓ 1 To reserve
2 Hello
3 Person
5 I am speaking

58

kärne	la carne	meat
pe'she	il pesce	fish
pō'lō ärō'stō	il pollo arrosto	roast chicken
dōō'e pō'lē ärō'stē	due polli arrosti	two roast chickens
pēzä	la pizza	pizza
menu del jōr'nō	il menu del giorno	today's special
tsōō'pä	la zuppa	soup
ōōnä tsōō'pä dē pe'she	una zuppa di pesce	fish soup
mēne'strä	la minestra	vegetable soup
dōō'e mēne'stre	due minestre	two vegetable soups
tōō'tō	tutto	all
bōō•on äpetē'tō	buon appetito	Enjoy your meal
kōn'tō	il conto	check
kōn'tō	il conto	check

Restaurants—meal times

Lunch, **il pranzo**, (largest meal of the day) is served from 12:00 to 3:00 P.M. Dinner, **la cena**, (less formal) is served after 8:00 P.M.

Pane et coperto

In Italian restaurants there is a small cover charge which includes the bread.

Tax receipt

Restaurant owners are required to issue a tax receipt (**ricevuta fiscale**). Save it because the tax authorities might check it.

Tips

The tip is usually already added to the check in the form of **il servizio**, or a 15% charge. Make sure it is included on your check before paying, if not (**servizio non compreso**), you should tip at least 10%–15% of the amount of the bill.

Parmesan cheese (**parmigiano**)

Grated cheese is served with soups, noodles, etc. at no extra charge.

12 At the Restaurant

_____?
What would you like?
_____, _____,
Meat, fish,
_____ _____, _____,
roast chicken, pizza,
__ ____ ___ _____?
today's special?

___ _____ _____,
Two roast chickens,
___ _____.
please.

12 At the Restaurant

→
1 Meat
2 Chicken
4 All
8 Fish
9 Pizza

↓
1 Check
3 Soup
5 Appetite
6 Menu
7 Vegetable soup

ke bēve'te	che bevete?	*What would you like to drink?*
ä'kōō•ä mēnerä'le	l'acqua minerale	*mineral water*
käpōōtshēnō	il cappuccino	*cappuccino*
lärän'tshätä	l'aranciata	*orange drink*
bē'rä	la birra	*beer*
vē'no rō'sō	il vino rosso	*red wine*
vē'nō ētälyä'nō	il vino italiano	*Italian wine*
skōō•ēzētō	squisito	*exquisite*

Price

At restaurants and bars, drinks are more expensive if you sit down at a table, and cheaper if you stand at the bar. However, once you have paid to drink at a table you are welcome to stay as long as you like. It is customary in an Italian bar or **Tavola Calda**, if you will be standing, to first place your order and pay at the cash register (**la cassa**) and then present your receipt (**lo scontrino**) to the barman (**il barista**). If you sit at a table you will be served by a waiter (**il cameriere**).

Italian wine

See page 100.

13 Drinks

14 Sick Malato

68

kō'me stä	come sta?	*How are you?*
mälä'to, mälä'tä	malato, malata	*sick*
ō	ho	*I have*
mäl dē te'stä	mal di testa	*headache*
mäl dē stō'mäkō	mal di stomaco	*stomach ache*
fe'bre	la febbre	*fever*
ō lä fe'bre	ho la febbre	*I have a fever*
o͞ona färmätshē'ä	una farmacia	*a pharmacy*
pästē'lyä	la pastiglia	*lozenge*
vōre'ē de'le	vorrei delle	*I'd like some*
pästel'yē	pastiglie	*lozenges*

The sign for an Italian pharmacy

14 Sick

71

I need a taxi!

tässē'	il tassi	*taxi*
kyämä're ōōn tässē'	chiamare un tassi	*to call a taxi*
pōtre'be kyämä're ōōn tässē'	potrebbe chiamare un tassi?	*Could you call a taxi?*
älä stätsyōn'ne	alla stazione	*to the station*
älä•erōpōrtō	all'aeroporto	*to the airport*
älōtel' ētälyä	all'hotel ITALIA	*to the Hotel ITALIA*
sē fermē	si fermi	*stop*
ōōn momen'tō	un momento	*one moment*
ventē mē'lä	ventimila	*twenty thousand*

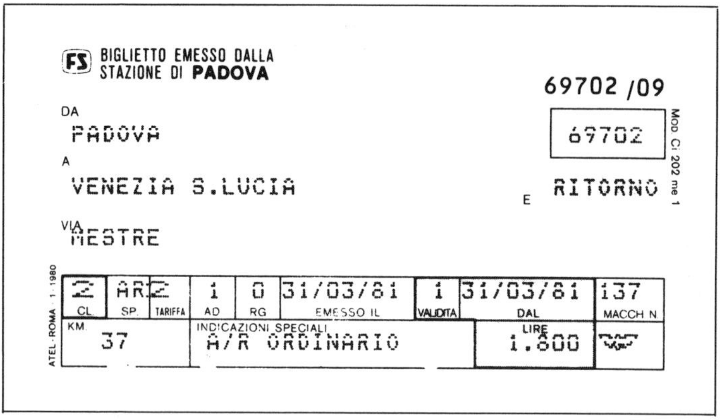

FS BIGLIETTO EMESSO DALLA
STAZIONE DI **PADOVA**

69702 /09

DA
PADOVA

67702

Mod Ci 202 me 1

A
VENEZIA S.LUCIA

E RITORNO

VIA
MESTRE

CL	SP.	TARIFFA	AD	RG	EMESSO IL	VALIDITA	DAL	MACCH N
2	AR	2	1	0	31/03/81	1	31/03/81	137

KM	INDICAZIONI SPECIALI	LIRE
37	A/R ORDINARIO	1.800

73

15 Taxi

Answers

Lesson 1

Buon giorno.

Mi faccia vedere il suo biglietto?
Il suo passaporto, per favore.

Il volo numero sedici parte
da quale porta?

Per New York?
Dalla porta numero due.

Quanti bagaglia ha?
Ho due.

Ecco il suo scontrino.
Ecco il suo passaporto.

Grazie, buon giorno.

Lesson 2

Vorrei noleggiare una macchina,
per favore.
Per quanto tempo?
Per una settimana.

Che tipo di macchina vorrebbe?
Una di lusso, a quattro porte.
Quanto costa?

Un milione duecentomila la settimana,
chilometre illimitati.

Bene, la prendo. Grazie.

Milano, Pavia, Genoa, Pisa, Firenze, Perugia, Viterbo, Roma

Lesson 3

Buona sera.
Buona sera, signore.

Ha una camera libera?
Si.
Una doppia.

Per quanto tempo?
Per cinque giorni.

Quanto costa la camera?

Centomila lire.

Bene.

La prendo.

5 CINQUE	1 GIORNO
6 CAMERA	2 QUANTO
7 LIRA	3 TEMPO
8 BENE	4 SERA

Lesson 4

Dov'è la sala da pranzo?
A destra, signora.

Buon giorno, signora.
Caffè, tè?
Caffelatte, per favore.

Ecco il caffè, i panini,
la confettura e il burro.

Un succo d'arancia?
Si.

2 SUCCO	1 BURRO
5 ARANCIA	3 CAFFÈ
7 SI	4 PANINO
8 COLAZIONE	6 SALA

Lesson 5

Vorrei una pianta della città, per favore . . .
Mille grazie.
Di niente!

Dov'è la galleria degli Uffizi?
Piazza della Signoria.

Lei può prendere un autobus.

Questo autobus va alla Piazza della Signoria?
Si.

Scusi, dov'è la Galleria degli Uffizi?
Non lo so.

A destra.
Grazie, Signore.

Vorrei un biglietto.

2 UFFIZI
3 SCUSI
5 GALLERIA
6 BIGLIETTO
7 VORREI
8 PIANTA

1 MILLE
4 CITTA

Lesson 6

Un espresso, per favore.

Fa molto caldo, oggi.

È americano?
Si, sono di New York.

Gli Stati Uniti sono belli.
Anche l'Italia.

Mi piace l'Italia,
il sole, il vino, l'arte.

Una sigaretta?
Mille grazie.

Lesson 7

Quanto costano gli occhiali da sole?
Cinquantamila lire.

Bene.
Li prendo.

Qualcosa d'altro?
No, grazie.

Dove potrei cambiare soldi?
Il "Banco di Roma" è là.

Buon giorno, signore.
Vorrei cambiare trecento dollari.

Il suo passaporto, per favore.
Sono trecentonovantamila lire.

Grazie. Buon giorno.

7 PASSAPORTO

1 COSA
2 LIRA
3 BANCO
4 CAMBIO
5 MONETA
6 VORREI

Lesson 8

Vorrei queste cartoline, per favore.
Duemila lire.

Ha anche francobolli?
No, signora,
la posta è là.

Quanto costa una cartolina per gli Stati Uniti?
Cinquecentocinquanta lire.

Cinque francobolli, per favore.

4 FRANCOBOLLO

1 CARTOLINA
2 ANCHE
3 POSTA

Lesson 9

Un gelato, per favore.
Vaniglia? Cioccolata? Fragole?

Vaniglia, per favore.

Un pedalò.
Quanto costa l'ora?
Ottomila lire.

È troppo caro.

Vorrei un ombrellone.
Quanto costa?
Trentamila lire.

Lo prendo.

Qualcosa d'altro?
Latte solare.

1 GELATO
2 SPIAGGIA
3 VANIGLIA
6 CIOCCOLATA

4 OMBRELLONE
5 LATTE
6 CARO

Lesson 10

Desidera?
Cinque arance.

Qualcosa d'altro?
Un chilo di pomodori.

Le banane sono molto buone.
No, grazie.

Qui abbiamo dell'aglio.
No, no!

Si.
L'aglio è molto buono per l'insalata di pomodori.

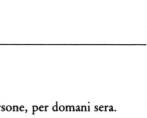

1 AGLIO
2 BANANA
3 ARANCIA
4 POMODORO

Lesson 11

Pronto.

Vorrei riservare una tavola per due persone, per domani sera.

Bene.
Il suo nome, per favore.

Il mio nome è Smith.

Smith? È americana?

Si, sono americana.

Buon giorno, signora.

4 SERA	1 RISERVARE
6 TAVOLA	2 PRONTO
7 DOMANI	3 PERSONA
8 NOME	5 PARLO

Lesson 12

Buona sera.
Una tavola per due persone.

Desidera?
Carne, pesce, pollo arrosto,
pizza, il menù del giorno?

Due polli arrosti, per favore.

Una zuppa? Zuppa di pesce?
Minestra?

Due minestre.
È tutto?

Ecco due polli arrosti.
Buon appetito.

Il conto, per favore.

1 CARNE	1 CONTO
2 POLLO	3 ZUPPA
4 TUTTO	5 APPETITO
8 PESCE	6 MENÙ
9 PIZZA	7 MINESTRA

Lesson 13

Che bevete?
Un'acqua minerale.
Un cappuccino.
Un'aranciata.

Una birra, per favore.
Un vino rosso, per favore.
Il vino rosso italiano è squisito.

| 3 CAPPUCCINO | 1 ACQUA |
| 4 ARANCIATA | 2 VINO |

Lesson 14

Buon giorno.
Buon giorno, Gina.

Come sta?
Sono malata.
Ho mal di testa.

Dov'è una farmacia?

Ho mal di testa.

Ho mal di stomaco.
Ho la febbre.

Vorrei delle pastiglie.

2 FEBBRE   1 TESTA
3 PASTIGLIA   2 FAMARCIA
4 STOMACO
5 MALATO

Lesson 15

Potrebbe chiamare un tassì, per favore.
Si, signore. Un momento.

Dove?
Alla stazione, per favore.

Si fermi qui.

Quanto costa?
Ventimila lire.

2 DOVE   1 HOTEL
4 AEROPORTO   3 TASSI
5 STAZIONE
6 ECCO

84

Syllable Puzzle

Puzzle on page 86

1. SO LE
2. BA NA NA
3. GE LA TO
4. OM BREL LO NE
5. CAF FE
6. SI GA RET TA
7. BIR RA
8. VI NO
9. PE SCE
10. TA VO LA
11. POL LO
12. PO MO DO RO
13. TE STA
14. LI RE
15. FRAN CO BOL LO
16. AU TO BUS
17. CAR TO LI NA

Food & Drink

Puzzle on page 90

TÈ
MENÙ
VINO
ACQUA
AGLIO
BIRRA
BURRO
CAFFÈ
CARNE
PESCE
PIZZA
POLLO

SUCCO
ZUPPA
GELATO
PANINO
ARANCIA
APPETITO
ESPRESSO
INSALATA
MINESTRA
POMODORO
CAPPUCCINO

Word-Building Puzzle

Puzzle on page 110

The Papal Palace:
CITTÀ DEL VATICANO

World-renowned Milanese opera house:
TEATRO ALLA SCALA

Italian artist and scholar:
LEONARDO DA VINCI

85

Syllable Puzzle

(Answers on page 84)

Form 17 words from these syllables and write them down. Picture clues and the number of syllables in each word are given on the next page.

AU	BA	BOL	BREL	BIR	BUS	CAF	CAR
CO	DO	FE	FRAN	GA	GE	LA	LA
LE	LI					LI	LO
LO	LO					MO	NA
NA	NA					NE	NO
OM	PE					PO	POL
RA	RE	RET	RO	SCE	SI	SO	STA
TA	TA	TE	TO	TO	TO	VI	VO

87

Mini-Dictionary for Tourists

English-Italian

Find the appropriate Italian word as needed.

a/an	un, una	*appetite*	appetito
abroad	all'estero	*appetizer*	antipasto
accelerator	acceleratore	*apple*	mela
accident	incidente	*apple juice*	succo de mela
address	indirizzo	*apple pie*	torta de mela
admission ticket	biglietto d'ingresso	*area code*	prefisso
after tomorrow	dopodomani	*arrival*	arriva
		arrivals	arrivi
afternoon	pomeriggio	*artichoke*	carciofo
air filter	filtro dell'aria	*ashtray*	portacenere
airplane	aero	*asparagus*	asparagi
airport service charge	aeroporto tassa d'embarco	*Australia*	Australia
		Australian	australiano
all	tutto		
always	sempre	*bacon*	lardo **B**
a lot	molto	*baggage claim*	consegna bagagli
ambulance	ambulanza	*bakery*	panetteria
America	America	*ball point pen*	biro
American	americano	*bank*	banca
and	e	*banknote*	banconota
anything	qualcosa	*barber*	parucchiere
		basilica	basilica

89

Food & Drink

(Answers on page 85)

23 Italian words related to food and drink appear in the diagram. They can be found horizontally or vertically. The 23 words are:

```
M I N E S T R A G V M
V C P I Z Z A R E E E
Z A V I N O G A L S N
O P E S C E L N A P U
I P O L L O I C T R A
S U C C O T O I O E P
A C Q U A E V A C S P
E C A F F E R I A S E
B I R R A B U R R O T
I N S A L A T A N E I
P O M O D O R O E L T
Z U P P A P A N I N O
```

bath	bagno	brandy	grappa
bathing shorts	calzoncini da bagno	bread	pane
		breakdown	guasto
bathing suit	costume da bagno	breakfast	prima colazione
bathroom	gabinetto	bridge	ponte
battery	pila, batteria	Britain	Gran Bretagna
beach	spiaggia	British	britannico
beach umbrella	ombrellone	broken	guasto
		broth	brodo
beans	fagioli	brown (chest-	marrone
beautiful	bello	nut brown)	
bed	letto	building	palazzo
beef	manzo	bus	autobus
beefsteak	bistecca	busy	occupato
beer	birra	butcher	macellaio
bell tower	campanile	butcher's shop	macelleria
belt	cintura		
bicycle	bicicletta	butter	burro
big	grande	buy	comprare
bikini	bikini	bye	ciao
bill	conto	cabbage	cavolo
bitter	amaro	café	pasticceria, caffè
black	negro		
blanket	coperta	cake	torta
blouse	camicetta	call	chiamare
blue	blu	camera	apparecchio fotografico
boarding house	penzione	camp site	campeggio
boat	barca	can opener	apriscatole
rent-a-boat	noleggiare una barca	cappuccino	cappuccino
		Canada	Canada
border	frontiera	Canadian	canadese
bottle	bottiglia	car	macchina, vettura
bottle opener	apribottiglie		
bow	arco	car rental	autonoleggio
box	scatola	carburetor	carburatore
braised	brasato	carafe	caraffa
brakes	freno	carrots	carrote

C

91

Fettuccine all'alfredo

Fettucine with cream and butter

12 ounces (340 g) fettucine	Cook pasta and drain.
2 cups (16 fluid ounces) light or heavy cream	Mix cream and egg yolks.
3–4 egg yolks	Melt butter in large pot, add cooked pasta, and mix well.
4 ounces (115 g) unsalted butter	
1-1/2 cups (170 g) grated Parmesan cheese	Add cream, egg yolks, grated cheese, salt & pepper to pasta.
Salt & freshly ground pepper to taste	Mix well.

cash register	cassa	cold	freddo
cauliflower	cavolfiore	collision	urto
cave	grotta	color	colore
centimeter	centimetro	comics	rivista
central station	statione centrale	consulate	consolato
		cookie	biscotto
change	cambio, cambiare	corkscrew	cavatappi
		corn meal mush	polenta
chassis	telaio		
cheap, inexpensive	a buon mercato, a buon prezo	coupon for gas	buono per benzina
		course (meal)	piatto
check	assegno	cover	coverto
cheese	formaggio	cover charge	coperta
cherry	ciliegia	croissant	brioche
cherry brandy	marascino	cucumbers	cetrioli
chicken	pollo	cup	tazza
chicory	chicorée	curve	curva
child	bambino	customs	dogana
chocolate	cioccolata	cutlet	costoletta
church	chiesa		
cigar	cigaro	danish	brioche
cigarette lighter	accendino	damage	danno
		danger	pericolo
city	città	day	giorno
map	pianta della città	dead (battery)	scarica
		deal	negozio
tour	giro della città	dealer	concessionario
		dear	caro
clock	orologio	decaffeinated	decaffeinato
closed	chiuso	deck	ponte
clothing	abbigliamento	deck chair	sedia a sdraio
cloudiness	nuvolosita	declare	dichiarare
clutch	frizione	defective	difettoso
coast	costa	degree	grado
cod	merluzzo	dent	urto
coffee	caffè	dentist	dentista
coffee with milk	caffelatte	department store	magazzino

D

Gamberi alla cacciatora

Shrimp Cacciatore

2 tablespoons (30 ml) butter	Melt butter in large pan.
1 pound (500 g) shrimp, peeled & deveined	Sauté shrimp with onion, green pepper and garlic.
1 small onion, chopped	
1 medium size green pepper, cut into strips	
1 clove garlic, minced	
28 ounces (190 g) whole tomatoes	Add tomatoes, tomato sauce, and seasonings.
8 ounces (225 g) tomato sauce	Bring to a full boil.
1/2 teaspoon (2 ml) oregano	
1/2 teaspoon (2 ml) basil	
1-1/2 cups (125 g) rice	Cook rice and drain. Add rice to shrimp and vegetable mixture and let stand 5 minutes. Fluff with fork and serve hot.

departure	partenza	emergency	emergenza
departures	partenze	England	Inghilterra
dessert	dosce	English	inglese
detour	deviazione	enjoy your	buon appetito
diesel	gasolio	meal	
dining car	carroza	entrance	entrata,
	ristorante		ingresso
dining room	sala da pranzo	espresso	espresso
dinner	pranzo	Eurocheque	Eurocheque
direct (train)	(treno) diretto	evening	sera
direction	directione	everything	tutto
discharge	scarica	excuse me	scusi
discount	riduzione	exhibition	esposizione
distance	distanza	exit	uscita
doctor	medico,	express train	direttissimo
	dottore		
dome	duomo	far	lontano
(cathedral)		farewell	addio
doors	porte	fast	veloce,
double bed	letto	(train)	presto,
	matrimoniale		subito
double room	doppia		(treno)
downtown	centro citta		rapido
dress	vestito	fender	parafengo
drink	bere	fennel	finocchio
drinks	bevande	ferry	traghetto
driver	autista	fever	febbre
driver's license	patente	fill out	riempire
drugstore	farmacia	film	pellicola
dynamo	dinamo	filter	filtro
		fire extin-	attrezzo
east	est	guisher	antincendio
eat	mangiare	firemen	pompieri
egg	uovo	first aid,	pronto
eggplant	melanzana	emergency	soccorso
elevator	ascensore	first floor	pianterreno
embarcation	imbarco	fish	pesce
embarcation	tassa		pescare
tax	d'imbarco	fish market	pescheria

F

95

Torta di Ricotta e spinaci

Spinach and Ricotta Pie

2 tablespoons (30 ml) butter	Melt butter in small skillet.
1 small onion, chopped	Sauté onions until tender.
1 10-ounce package (285 g) frozen chopped spinach, thawed	Drain spinach in sieve and press with spoon to remove all liquid.
1 pound (500 g) ricotta cheese 1/2 cup (55 g) Parmesan cheese 2 eggs, beaten 1/4 teaspoon (1 ml) garlic salt 1/4 teaspoon (1 ml) white pepper 1/4 teaspoon (1 ml) ground nutmeg	Combine spinach, sautéed onions, ricotta cheese, Parmesan cheese, eggs, and seasonings in medium size bowl. Mix well.
1 9-inch (22 cm) unbaked pie shell	Preheat oven to 375° (190°C). Spoon into pie shell and bake for 45 minutes. Serve hot.

fix	riparare	*glass*	bicchiere
flashlight	flash, pila	*glasses*	occhiali
flight	volo	*go*	andare
flyer	opuscolo	*gold*	oro
fog	nebbia	*golf*	golfo
food	alimentari	*gondola*	gondola
for	per	*good*	buono
forbidden	viettato	*good bye*	arrivederci
foreign currency	estero valuta	*good day*	buon giorno
		good evening	buona sera
fork	forchetta	*goulash*	spezzatino
form	modulo	*gram*	grammo
fountain	fontana	*grape juice*	succo d'uva
fourth	quarto	*grapefruit*	pompelmo
free	libero	*grated*	grattugiato
french fries	patate fritte	*green*	verde
Friday	venerdi	*green salad*	insalata verde
fridge	frigorifero	*grey*	grigio
fried	fritto	*ground floor*	pianterreno
fruit	frutto	*guarded*	custotido
juice	succo di frutta	*guide*	guida
		guided tour	visita guida
salad	macedonia	*gulf*	golfo
fruit in season	frutta di stazione		
		hair-stylist	parrucchiere
full	pieno	*half*	mezzo
fuse	fusibile	*half bottle*	mezzo bottiglia
gallery	galleria	*half hour*	mezzo ora
garage	garage	*ham (boiled)*	prosciutto cotto
gas	benzina		
pedal	accelerator	*hammer*	martello
unleaded	senza piombo (benzina verde)	*handbag*	borsa
		handkerchief	fazzoletto
		hat	cappello
		head	testa
gate	uscita	*headache*	mal di testa
gearshift	cambio delle marce	*heart attack*	infarto, attaco cardiaco

H

97

Pasta Carbonara

Pasta in cream sauce with egg and ham

1/2 onion, chopped *Olive oil* *1/2 pound bacon or smoked ham*	Sauté chopped onion in oil. Cut bacon or ham into small chunks and fry with onions. When cooked, strain off oil and fat and return to burner.
4 cups (1 L) heavy cream *1 pinch salt and pepper* *1 pinch chopped fresh parsley*	Add heavy cream with salt, pepper and fresh parsley. Let mixture cook until it boils.
Linguine or spaghetti *2 egg yolks, beaten* *3 tablespoons (45 ml) grated cheese*	Cook pasta and strain. Put back into pot. Add beaten egg yolks. Stir for 2–3 minutes. Add cream mixture and mix well. Add grated cheese, stir 2–3 minutes more and serve.

help	aiuto	*juice*	succo	
here is	ecco	*July*	luglio	
hi	ciao	*key*	chiave	K
high pressure	alta pressione	*kilogram*	chilo	
highway	autostrada	*kilometer*	chilometro	
his/her	suo	*knife*	coltello	
honey	miele	*lake*	lago	L
hospital	ospedale	*lamb*	agnello	
hotel	albergo	*last name*	cognome	
house	casa	*lawyer*	avvocato	
how much	quanto	*lead*	piombo	
hunter	cacciatore	*lemon*	limone	
ice	ghiaccio	*lemonade*	limonata	
ice cream	gelato	*letter*	lettera	
(*parlor*)	(gelateria)	*license*	patente	
(*cake*)	(cassata)	*license plate*	targa	
(*dish*)	(coppa)	*light*	accendere	
icy (*road*)	ghiacciata	*lighter*	accendino	
	(strada)	*like* (*I'd*)	vorrei	
ignition	accensione	*liquor*	liquore	
indigestion	indigestione	*liter*	litro	
information	informazione	*little*	piccolo	
injured	ferito	*liver*	fegato	
innocent	innocente	*local train*	treno locale	
insurance	assicurazione	*lodging*	alloggio	
(*card*)	(carta verde)	*long*	lungo	
interpreter	interprete	*lose*	perdere	
Ireland	Irlanda	*low pressure*	pressione	
Irish	irlandese		bassa	
island	insel	*lozenge*	pastiglia	
Italy	Italia	*luggage*	bagagli, valigie	
Italian	italiano	*lunch*	pranzo	
it is necessary	bisogna	*luxury*	di lusso	
to		*Madam, Mrs.*	signora	M
		magazine	rivista	
jack	cricco	*mail*	posta	
jacket	giacca	*mail box*	buca delle	
jam	confeturra		lettere	

99

BARBERA D'ASTI

DENOMINAZIONE DI ORIGINE CONTROLLATA

75cl. e | **1983** | BOTTIGLIA NUMERATA
№ 102647

IMBOTTIGLIATO DA:
AZIENDA VINICOLA ALBESE - PRIOCCA D'ALBA
ITALIEN

The best known Italian wines are produced in the following regions:

Famous Wines:

Tuscany	Chianti, Chianti classico . . .
Piedmont	Barbera, Barolo, Barbaresco . . .
Emilia-Romagna	Lambrusco, Albana . . .
Trentino-Alto-Adige	Lago di Caldaro, Maddalena . . .
Latium	Frascati, Marino . . .
Sicily	Marsala, Corvo . . .

Melini®
Chianti Classico
DENOMINAZIONE DI ORIGINE CONTROLLATA E GARANTITA

0,750 ℓ e IMBOTTIGLIATO NELLE PROPRIE CANTINE DI GAGGIANO DA
MELINI S.p.A. - POGGIBONSI 12%VOL.
ITALIA

100

man	uomo	*mountain*	montagna, monte
map	carta		
mark	marco	*mountain climbing*	alpinismo
market	mercato		
marmelade	marmellata	*Mrs.*	signora
matches	fiammiferi	*municipality*	comune
maximum speed	velocita massima	*mural*	affresco
		museum	museo
meal	buon appetito	*mushrooms*	funghi
have a nice meal		*mussels*	cozze
		mustard	mustarda
meat	carne	*my*	mio
melon	melone		
meter	metro	*name*	nome
midday	mezzogiorno	*napkin*	tovagliolo
milk	latte	*nation*	paese
milk shake	frullato	*nationality*	nazionalità
mineral water	acqua minerale	*newspaper*	giornale
		nice	gentile
mint	menta	*night*	notte
minute	minuto	*no*	no
mirror	specchio	*noon*	mezzogiorno
Miss	signorina	*normal*	normale
mist	foschia	*north*	nord
Mister, Mr.	signore	*nothing*	niente, nulla
mixed	misto	*number*	numero
moment	momento	*nut*	nocciola, nocce
Monday	lunedi		
money	denaro		
month	mese	*offer*	offerta
moped	ciclomotore	*office*	ufficio
morning	mattina	*oil*	olio
mosquito	zanzara	*change*	cambio d'olio
motel	motel		
motor	motore	*level*	livello dell'olio
boat	motoscafo		
cycle	motocicletta	*pump*	pompa dell'olio
oil	olio motore		
motor home	roulotte	*okay*	va bene

N

O

101

Cariciofi ripieni — *Stuffed Artichokes*

4 artichokes	Trim artichoke tops and stems. Pull off tough outer leaves. Rinse under cold water. Bang on table to spread leaves open.
1/2 cup (4 fluid ounces) olive oil	Combine all remaining ingredients.
1 cup (85 g) bread crumbs	Sprinkle mix in between open leaves.
1/2 cup (55 g) grated Parmesan cheese	Place upright in roasting pan. Fill pan with 1/2 inch (1 cm) water.
2 tablespoons (30 ml) freshly chopped parsley	Cover with aluminum foil and steam for 1/2 hour on stove.
4 cloves garlic, minced	
Salt and pepper to taste	

olive	oliva	*pig*	maiale
omelet	frittata	*pillow*	cuscino
one way	senso unico	*pistachio*	pistacchio
open	aperto	*plate*	piatto
opera	opera	*police*	polizia
orange	succo	*pool*	piscina
orange juice	succo	*pork*	maiale
	d'arrancia	*port*	porto
outing	gita	*postcard*	cartolina
		post office	posta
package	pacco	*potatoes*	patate
painting	quadro	*prefix*	prefisso
palace	pallazo	*press*	spingere
pants	pantaloni	*price*	prezzo
paper	carta	*price list*	elenco dei
parking	parcheggio		prezzi
parking pass	disco orario	*private*	privato
("*disk*")		*prohibited*	proibito
Parmesan	parmigiane	*pull*	tirare
cheese		*push*	springere
pass	passo		
passport	passaporto	*quarter*	quarto
passport check	controllo		
	passporti	*rabbit*	coniglio
pasta	pasta	*radiator*	radiatore
pastries	pasticcini	*railroad*	ferrovia
pay	pagare	*rain*	pioggia
payment	pagamento	*razor*	rasoio
peach	pesca	*receipt*	ricevuta
pear	pera	*red*	rosso
peas	piselli	*red wine*	vino rosso
pedal boat	pedalo	*reduction*	riduzione
pepper	pepe	*registration*	immatricol-
peppers	peperoni		zione
photograph	foto	*refrigerator*	frigorifero
picture	fotografare	*regular gas*	benzina
(*take a*)			normale
pie	torte	*rent*	noleggiare
piece	pezzo	*repair*	reparazione

Q

R

103

Pasta Allizalata   *Pasta Salad*

8 Italian tomatoes, peeled & diced	Mix tomatoes, garlic, and basil in bowl.
3 cloves garlic, chopped	
3 basil leaves, crushed	
1/4 cup (2 fluid ounces) olive oil	Add oil, salt, and red pepper.
1 teaspoon (5 ml) salt	Stir until blended.
1 pinch crushed red pepper	
Pasta of your choice	Cook pasta and reserve about one cup of cooking water in pot with pasta. Add tomato mixture, stir and then serve.

report (someone to the police)	denuncia (fare una denuncia)	shock absorber	ammortizzatore
reservation	prenotazione	shoes	scarpe
rest rooms	gabinetto	short	corto
restaurant	trattoria	short circuit	corto circuito
rice	riso	shower	doccia
right (on/to the)	destra (a destra)	sick	malato
river	fiume	side dishes	contorni
road	strada	sightseeing tour	visita guidata
roast	arrosto	sign	firmare
roast veal	vitello arrosto	signature	firma
rob	rubare	single room	camera singola
rolls	panini	size, cut	taglia, misura
room	camera	skirt	gonna
		sleep	dormire
salt	sale	sleeping car	carrozze cuccette
sanitary napkin	assorbenti igienici	sleeping pills	somniferi
sardine	sardine	sleeve	manica
Saturday	sabato	slide	diapositiva
sauce	salsa	slow	lento
schedule	orario	slow down	ralentare
Scotland	Scozia	snow	neve
Scottish	scozzese	snow chains	catena da neve
screwdriver	cacciavite	soap	sapore
sea	mare	socks	calzini
seafood	frutti di mare	soft drink	bibita
season	stagione	sole	sogliola
seat	sedia	something	qualcosa
seatbelt	cintura di sicurezza	soup	zuppa
		south	sud
service	servizio	spare tire	ruota di scorta
service area	area di servizio	spark plug	candela
		spare part	pezzo di ricambio
service station	statione di servizio	sparkling wine	spumante
		special offer	offerta speciale

World-Famous Italian Cheeses

Name:	Use:
Parmesan cheese (Parmigiano) hard cheese, strong flavor. Keeps several months. You can also grate: **Asiago, Pecorino.**	Parmesan cheese is grated and sprinkled on noodle and rice dishes. Also suitable for sauces.
Bel Paese Semi-soft cutting cheese from cow's milk. Tastes slightly sour. Keeps 1–2 weeks.	Suitable for pizza, baking.
Gorgonzola Blue mold cheese. Tastes sweetish/spicy. Keeps 1 week.	Crumbled in sauces and tossed salads.
Mozzarella Fresh white cheese, moist, dripping. Mozzarella melts easily. Tastes slightly sweet/sour. Keeps 1–2 weeks in brine.	Suitable for pizza and tossed salads.

specialty	specialita della casa	*sunburn*	scottatura solare
speed	velocita	*Sunday*	domenica
spinach	spinaci	*sunglasses*	occhiali da sole
spire	campanile		
spoon	cucchiaio	*suntan creme*	crema solare
square	piazza	*suntan lotion*	latte solare
stamp	francobollo	*super*	super
starter	starter, motorino d'avvia- mento	*supermarket*	supermercato
		supper	cena
		sweater	pullover
station	stazione	*sweets*	dolce
(*main*)	centrale	*swim*	nuotare
statue	statua	*swimming pool*	piscina
steal	rubare		
steering wheel	volante	*table*	tavola T
stewed		*table wine*	vino di tavola
meat	brasato	*tank*	bombola
apples	composte	*tariff*	tariffa
stockings	calze	*taxi*	tassi
stomach	stomaco	*tea*	te
stomach ache	mal di stomaco	*telegram*	telegramma
		telephone	telefono
stool	sedia	*telephone book*	elenco telefonico
stop	fermata		
(*bus*)	(dell' autobus)	*telephone token*	gettone
(*no*)	divieto di		
stop(ping)	sosta	*temple*	tempio
store	negozio	*tennis*	tennis
storm	temporale	*tennis court*	campo di tennis
straight ahead	sempre diritto		
strawberries	fragole	*tent*	tenda
street	via, strada	*terrace*	terrazza
string beans	fagiolini	*thank you*	grazie
strong	forte	*the*	il, la
sugar	zucchero	*theater*	teatro
suitcase	valiglia	*theft*	furto
sun	sole	*they*	lei

Numbers

0	zero	80	ottanta
1	uno	90	novanta
2	due	100	cento
3	tre	120	cento venti
4	quattro	200	duecento
5	cinque	300	trecento
6	sei	400	quattrocento
7	sette	500	cinquecento
8	otto	600	seicento
9	nove	700	settecento
10	dieci	800	ottocento
11	undici	900	novecento
12	dodici	1 000	mille
13	tredici	2 000	duemila
14	quattordici	3 000	tremila
15	quindici	5 000	cinquemila
16	sedici	10 000	diecimila
17	diciassette	20 000	ventimila
18	diciotto	50 000	cinquantamila
19	diciannove	100 000	centomila
20	venti	500 000	cinquecentomila
21	ventuno	1 000 000	un milione
22	ventidue		
23	ventitré		
28	ventotto		
29	ventinove		
30	trenta		
31	trentuno		
32	trentadue		
33	trentatré		
40	quaranta		
50	cinquanta		
60	sessanta		
70	settanta		

this	questo	*van*	camionetta
thread	filo	*vanilla*	vaniglia
Thursday	giovedi	*veal*	vitello
ticket	biglietto	*veal cacciatore*	vitello
ticket box office	biglietteria		cacciatore
tights	collant	*veal cutlet*	saltimbocca
tobacconist	tabaccheria	*veal shank*	ossobucco
tobacco shop	tabaccheria	*vegetables*	verdura
today's special	piatto del	*vegetable soup*	minestra
	giorno	*(with pasta)*	minestrone
toilet (rest rooms)	toilette, gabinetto	*vendor*	venditore
toll	pedaggio	*vehicle*	veicolo
tomato	pomodoro	*vermouth*	vermut
tomato juice	succo di	*very soon*	fra poco
	pomodoro	*vinegar*	aceto
toothpaste	dentrifricio	*vineyard*	vino nostramo
tourist	touristo	*visit*	visitare
tourist office	aziendi di	*volcano*	vulcano
	soggiorno		
tower	torre	*waiter*	cameriere **W**
towing service	soccorso	*Wales*	Galles
	stradale	*walk*	camminare
traffic light	semaforo	*wallet*	portafoglio
train (on/in the)	treno (in treno)	*warm*	caldo
trout	trota	*warning triangle*	triangolo
Tuesday	martedi	*water*	acqua
tuna	tono	*weather*	tempo
turn on	accendere	*weather forecast*	previsone del tempo
umbrella	ombrella	*Wednesday*	mercoledi
United States	Stati Uniti	*week*	settimana
unlimited	illimitato	*Welsh*	gallese
		welcome	benvenuto
valley	valle	*west*	ovest
valuable objects	oggetti	*what*	cosa
		wheel	ruota, pneumatico
		when	quando

109

Word-Building Puzzle

(Answers on page 85)

Write the letters of the Italian words in the boxes as indicated. For example, if the number "2" appears, write the second letter of the word suggested by the picture.

The Papal Palace:

5.6.   7.8.9.   5.   2.3.   3.6.   4.5.   1.2.   3.4.

☐☐☐☐☐☐   ☐☐☐☐   ☐☐☐☐☐☐☐☐

World-renowned Milanese opera house:

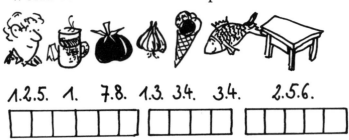

1.2.5.   1.   7.8.   1.3.   3.4.   3.4.   2.5.6.

☐☐☐☐☐☐   ☐☐☐☐☐   ☐☐☐☐☐☐

Italian artist and scholar:

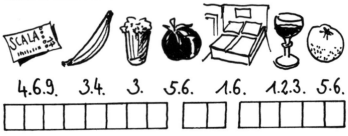

4.6.9.   3.4.   3.   5.6.   1.6.   1.2.3.   5.6.

☐☐☐☐☐☐☐☐   ☐☐☐   ☐☐☐☐☐

where	dove	*woolen jacket*	giacca de lana
white	bianco	*work*	lavoro
white wine	vino bianco	*wrench*	chiave inglese
wide	largo		
wife	moglie	*year*	anno
wind	vento	*yellow*	giallo
wine	vino	*yes*	si
windshield	tergicristallo	*yesterday*	ieri
windshield wipers	parabrezza tergicristallo	*youth hostel*	ostello della gioventu
wire	filo		
with	con	*zip code*	codice di avviamento postale (C.A.P.)
without	senza		
witness	testimone		
woman	donna		
wool	lana	*zucchini*	zuchini

Y

Z

Useful Addresses:

American Embassy
Via Vittorio Veneto, 119A
00187 Rome
(06) 46 74

American Consulate
Largo Donegani 1
20121 Milan
(02) 65 28 41

Canadian Embassy
Via G.B. de Rossi, 27
00161 Rome
(06) 85 53 41

Canadian Consulate-General
Via Vittor Pisani, 19
20124 Milan
(02) 669 74 51

British Embassy
Via XX Settembre, 80A
00187 Rome
(06) 475 54 41/ 475 55 51

British Consulate-General
Via San Paolo, 7
20121 Milan
(02) 869 34 42

Australian Embassy
Via Alessandria, 215
00198 Rome
(06) 83 27 21

Australian Consulate-General
Via Turati, 40
20121 Milan
(02) 659 87 27